EGYPT'S Ancient Secrets

GHOST SHIP

The Pharaoh's Buried Vessel

by Ruth Owen

Consultant: Dr. Christopher Naunton
Egyptologist

BEARPORT PUBLISHING

New York, New York

Credits

Cover and Title Page, © Jeff Schultes/Shutterstock and © Gilles Gaonach/Shutterstock; 4, © Bettmann/Getty Images; 4–5, © Danita Delmont/Shutterstock and © Planner/Shutterstock; 6L, © Jack Sullivan/Alamy; 6R, © Manna Nader/Gabana Studios Cairo; 7, © age fotostock/Alamy; 8, © Mike Fuckslocher/iStock Photo; 9T, © Christine Osborne Pictures/Alamy; 9B, © Noppharat4569/Shutterstock; 10, © Popperfoto/Getty Images; 11T, © Valentyn Volkov/Shutterstock, © Anna Sedneva/Shutterstock, and © oksana2010/Shutterstock; 11B, © Granger Historical Picture Archive/Alamy; 12L, © World History Archive/Alamy; 12R, © Magica/Alamy; 12B, © Mark Millmore; 13, © Granger Historical Picture Archive/Alamy; 14L, © Empire331/Dreamstime; 14R, Public Domain; 15, Public Domain; 16T, © Manna Nader/Gabana Studios Cairo; 16B, © Danita Delimont/Alamy; 17T, © Ken Backer/Dreamstime; 17B, Public Domain; 18, © Ian Patrick/Alamy; 19, © age fotostock/Alamy; 20, © Jeff Schultes/Shutterstock; 21T, © Alison Wright/Getty Images; 21B, © DEA/F. GUENET/Getty Images; 22, © Stock Connection Blue/Alamy; 22–23, © sculpies/Shutterstock; 23B, © De Agostini Picture Library/Getty Images; 24, © epa european pressphoto agency b.v./Alamy; 25T, © ZUMA Press, Inc./Alamy; 25BL, © Amanda Lewis/Dreamstime; 26, © Alex Zarubin/Dreamstime; 27, Public Domain; 28, © David Kerkhoff/Istock Photo; 29T, Public Domain; 29B, © Kokhanchikov/Shutterstock; 31, © De Agostini Picture Library/Getty Images.

Publisher: Kenn Goin
Senior Editor: Joyce Tavolacci
Creative Director: Spencer Brinker
Photo Researcher: Ruby Tuesday Books Ltd

Library of Congress Cataloging-in-Publication Data

Names: Owen, Ruth, 1967– author.
Title: Ghost ship : the pharaoh's buried vessel / by Ruth Owen.
Other titles: Egypt's ancient secrets.
Description: New York, New York : Bearport Publishing Company, 2017. | Series: Egypt's ancient secrets | Includes bibliographical references and index.
Identifiers: LCCN 2016049176 (print) | LCCN 2016051600 (ebook) | ISBN 9781684020270 (library) | ISBN 9781684020799 (ebook)
Subjects: LCSH: Royal Ship of Cheops—Juvenile literature. | Wooden boats—Egypt—Juvenile literature. | Egypt—Civilization—To 332 B.C.—Juvenile literature. | Excavations (Archaeology)—Egypt—Jåizah—Juvenile literature.
Classification: LCC DT62.S55 O94 2017 (print) | LCC DT62.S55 (ebook) | DDC 932/.012—dc23
LC record available at https://lccn.loc.gov/2016049176

Copyright © 2017 Bearport Publishing Company, Inc. All rights reserved. No part of this publication may be reproduced in whole or in part, stored in any retrieval system, or transmitted in any form or by any means, electronic, mechanical, photocopying, recording, or otherwise, without written permission from the publisher.

For more information, write to Bearport Publishing Company, Inc.,
45 West 21st Street, Suite 3B, New York, New York 10010.
Printed in the United States of America.

10 9 8 7 6 5 4 3 2 1

Contents

Discovery in the Desert

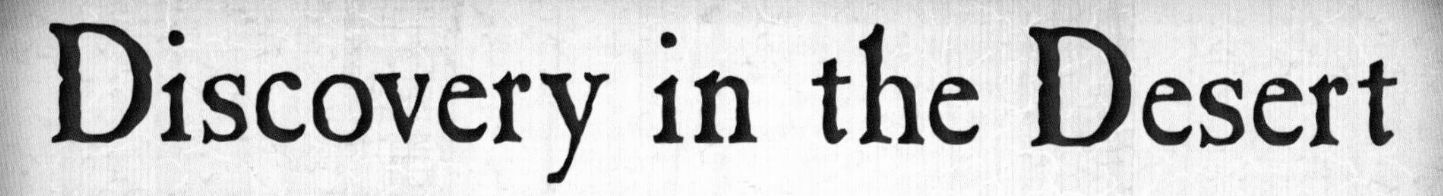

It was a scorching spring morning in May 1954. **Archaeologist** Kamal Al-Mallakh was hard at work **excavating** a site in the Egyptian desert. A few weeks before, workers had made a thrilling discovery near the base of the Great Pyramid of Giza. They had found 41 huge stone blocks joined with **plaster** buried under the sand and rock.

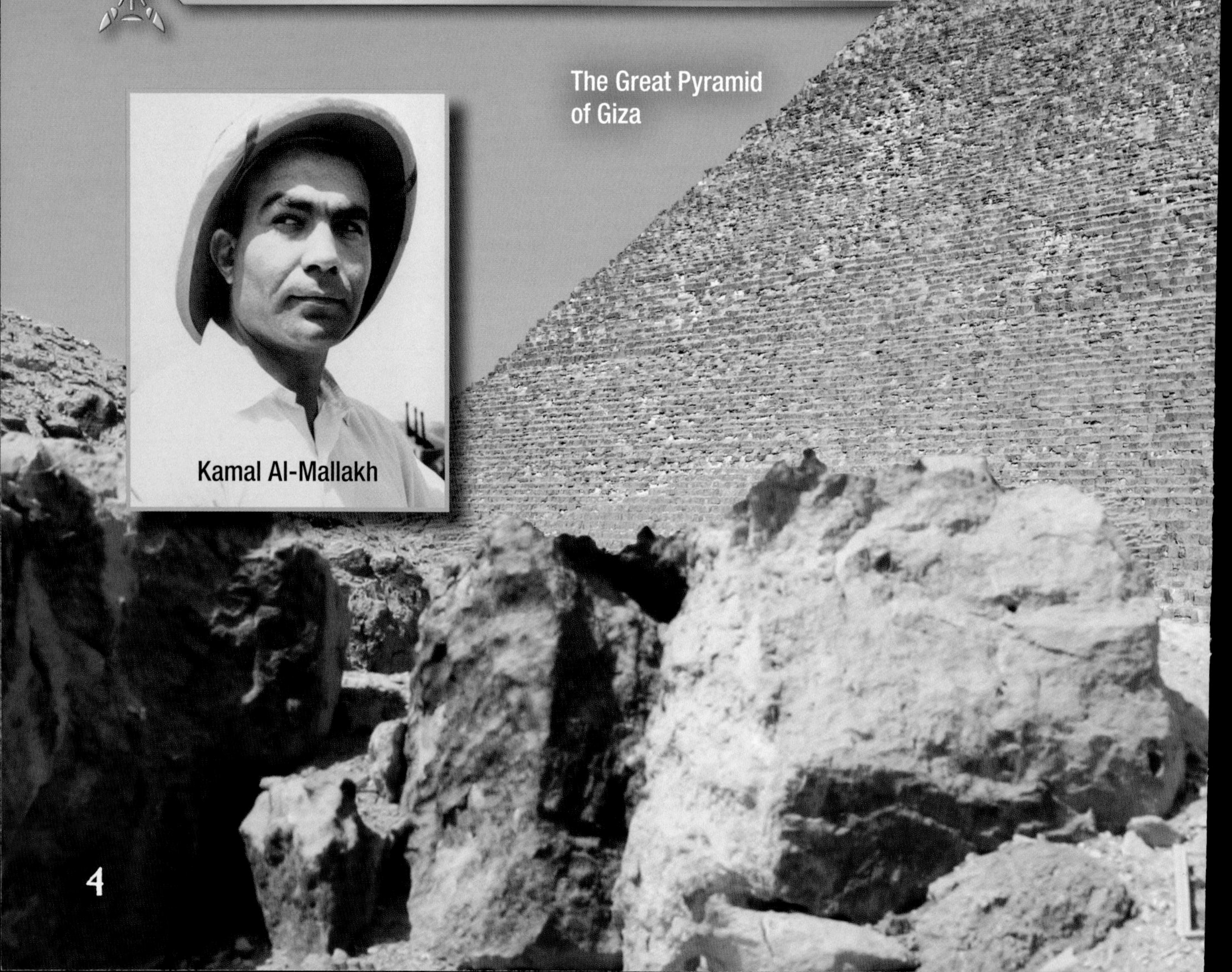

The Great Pyramid of Giza

Kamal Al-Mallakh

As Al-Mallakh chipped away at the plaster, he was filled with excitement. He hoped the blocks were covering ancient Egyptian **artifacts**. Finally, Al-Mallakh created a tiny hole in the plaster. He held up a small mirror to capture a beam of sunlight. Then he directed the light into the hole and peered into the darkness.

The Great Pyramid of Giza was built as a **tomb** for the ancient Egyptian king **Pharaoh** Khufu. The pyramid took up to 20 years to build. It was completed around 2560 B.C.—that's more than 4,500 years ago!

The World's Oldest Ship

As Al-Mallakh looked into the tiny black hole, the strong smell of wood filled his nose. Beneath the stone blocks, there was a large, dark pit. He flashed the beam of light from the mirror around in the darkness. Suddenly, he saw a long wooden **oar** . . . and, beneath the oar, large pieces of **timber**. Al-Mallakh had found a wooden ship! In fact, he'd discovered the world's oldest surviving ship.

Stone blocks

Dark pit beneath blocks

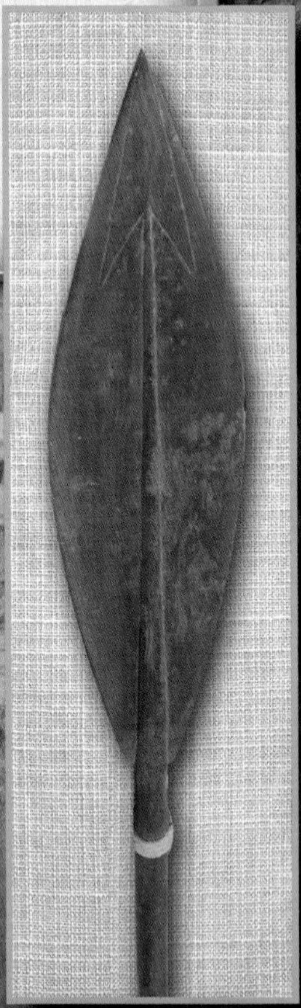

One of the ship's wooden oars

Al-Mallakh believed the wooden ship had been built for Pharaoh Khufu. Then, after the pharaoh died, it was buried alongside his pyramid. Now, more than 4,500 years later, Al-Mallakh had found the incredible **vessel**. Yet why would an Egyptian pharaoh need a ship in a hot, dry desert?

In the past, other boat-shaped pits had been discovered alongside the Great Pyramid. When archaeologists opened up these pits, however, they were empty.

An empty boat-shaped pit alongside the Great Pyramid

Who Were the Ancient Egyptians?

The ancient Egyptians were a **civilization** based in Africa from around 3000 B.C. to A.D. 300. Even though they lived in a desert, the ancient Egyptians were skillful boat builders and sailors. That's because they built their kingdom along a large waterway called the River Nile.

The River Nile is 4,258 miles (6,853 km) long. It flows north and empties into the Mediterranean Sea.

Like a watery highway, the Nile was the main route for people in ancient Egypt to travel around. The river was important in other ways, too. In Egypt, it hardly ever rains. So the ancient Egyptians relied on the river for drinking water. It also provided them with food, including fish, turtles, and waterbirds. In addition, the people gathered **papyrus** plants that grew along the river.

What ancient Egyptian fishermen and their papyrus boats might have looked like

Papyrus plants

The ancient Egyptians used papyrus to make paper, sandals, and baskets. They also tied together bundles of papyrus stems to make small boats.

The Nile—Giver of Life

The River Nile did more than provide the ancient Egyptians with food and papyrus. It also made it possible for them to grow crops. Every year, heavy rains fell in an area south of Egypt called Ethiopia. The rains created a **torrent** of water that flowed north along the Nile into Egypt. The river overflowed its banks and flooded the land, bringing **nutrients** to the soil. This created **fertile** areas on either side of the river that were ideal for growing different crops.

Floodwaters in Egypt

In the rich soil, the ancient Egyptians planted wheat for bread and barley for making beer. In addition, they grew onions, cabbages, beans, grapes, figs, and pomegranates. They also grew a plant called flax, which they turned into linen for making clothes.

The ancient Egyptians had three seasons. The season of Akhet (June to September) was the flood season. Peret (October to February) was the growing season. Finally, Shemu (March to May) was the harvesting season.

This painting shows ancient Egyptian farmers at work.

Life on the Nile

Just as today's roads are filled with different vehicles, the Nile in ancient Egypt was crowded with many kinds of boats. Fishermen threw out their nets from small papyrus boats. People traveled around Egypt on large, wooden ferries. Still bigger ships called barges carried food, timber, and other goods to different places.

An ancient Egyptian ferry

Ancient Egyptian fishermen standing in a papyrus boat

The pharaoh and royal family also sailed on barges. The passengers sat under a **canopy** to shield them from the hot sun.

This illustration shows how a royal barge may have looked.

In fact, many of the huge stones used to build Pharaoh Khufu's pyramid were transported by barges. These giant barges had crews of up to 500 sailors. Chunks of granite that weighed up to 55 tons (50 metric tons) were loaded onto the barges at **quarries** and then moved along the river. Sometimes the barges were towed by teams of men. The men walked along the riverbank, pulling on ropes that were attached to the barge. Other ancient Egyptian boats had sails and a crew of people who rowed the vessel with oars.

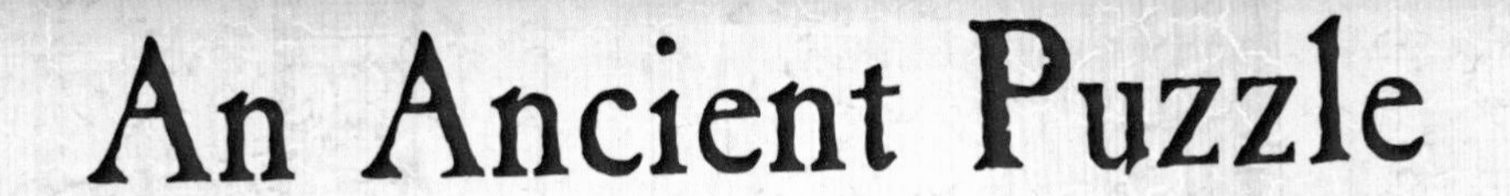

An Ancient Puzzle

Boats were a very important part of everyday life in ancient Egypt. Over the years, archaeologists had discovered small models and paintings of boats inside the tombs of pharaohs and other important Egyptians. Finding an actual life-size ancient Egyptian ship was very unusual, however.

It took Al-Mallakh and a team of workers about 18 months to carefully remove the huge stone blocks that covered the large boat pit. Inside the hole, they found a giant pile of wooden pieces.

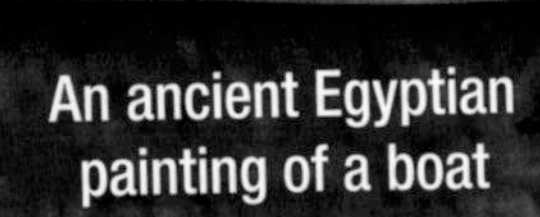

An ancient Egyptian painting of a boat

Pieces of the ship inside the pit

They quickly noticed that the ship was carefully laid out like a giant puzzle. The ancient Egyptian workers who had buried the ship had taken it apart before placing it in the pit. In total, Al-Mallakh's team found 1,224 pieces of wood. Unfortunately, the ship was not buried with any instructions for how to put it together. In order to bring the ancient ship back to life, someone would have to figure out how to **reconstruct** it!

Ancient Egyptian rope

Some pieces of the ship were 66 feet (20 m) long. Others measured just a few inches. The pit also contained dozens of feet of rope and 12 wooden oars.

Stepping Back in Time

Who would rebuild the ancient ship? The person given the difficult task was Haj Ahmed Youssef. Youssef was an expert in **restoring** ancient artifacts, but he had never rebuilt an ancient Egyptian boat.

Youssef carefully studied old Egyptian carvings, paintings, and models of boats. He also watched modern-day Egyptian boat builders at work. Finally, he was ready to begin the huge task of rebuilding the 4,500-year-old ship, piece by piece.

Haj Ahmed Youssef

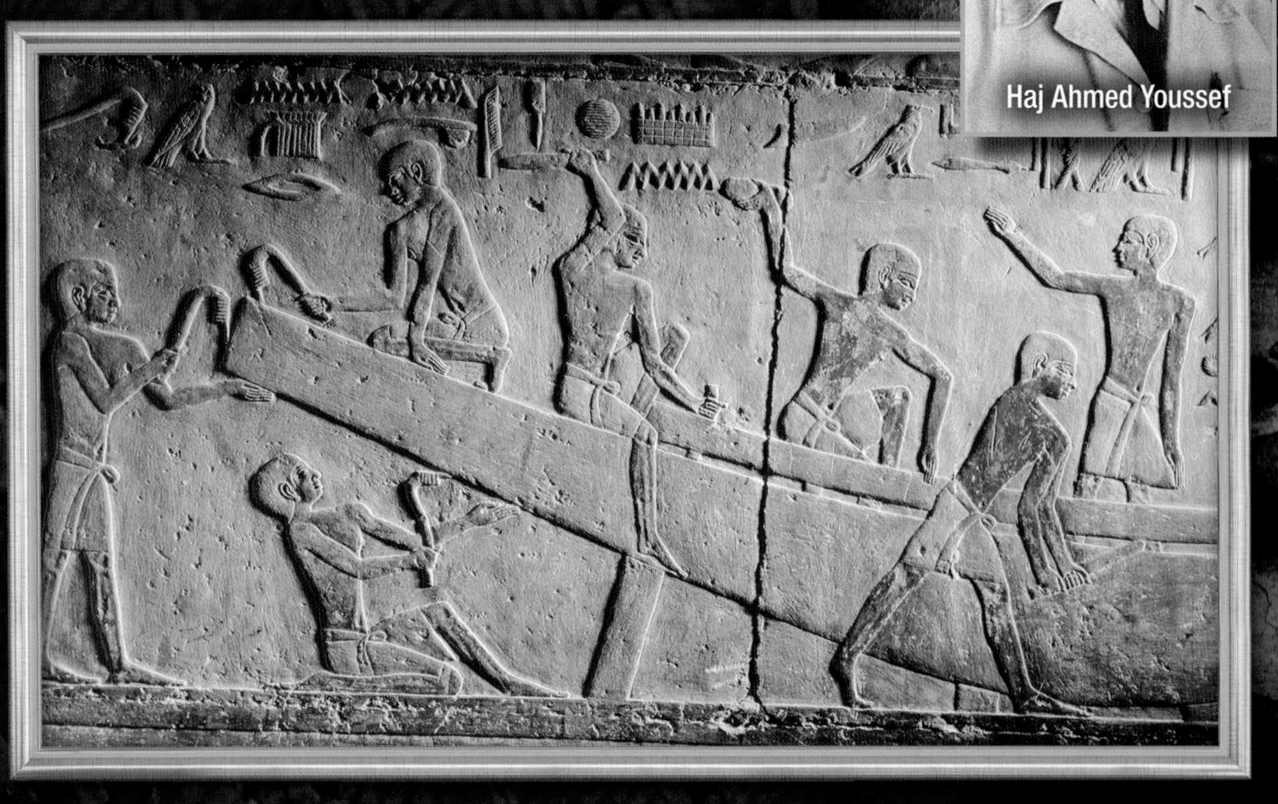

This rock carving from a tomb shows ancient Egyptian boat builders at work.

In the Egyptian desert, there were no trees with tall, straight trunks for making long planks of wood. Youssef and a team of scientists discovered that the cedar wood used to build the boat had been transported hundreds of miles from a country called Lebanon.

Youssef soon learned just how skillful the ancient carpenters were. Using only very basic tools made of copper and a rock called flint, they carefully shaped the cedar timbers so they locked together.

When Al-Mallakh first looked into the pit, he smelled cedar wood. Even though the boat had been buried for thousands of years, the ancient wood had not lost its strong scent.

An Egyptian tool made of flint

A team of restorers rebuilding the ship

Sewing Up the Pieces

Youssef not only had to learn how to be an ancient carpenter. He also had to learn to sew—with rope! Ancient Egyptian shipbuilders didn't use nails to join pieces of timber. Instead, they carved thousands of V-shaped cuts into the wood. Then they tightly wound rope into the cuts to lash the pieces of wood together. The process of tying the wood with rope was a little like sewing. So boat builders in ancient Egypt were often known as "boat sewers."

This is a model section of the Khufu ship. It's possible to

Once the ancient boat builders placed the ship in water, the wet wood swelled up and the ropes shrunk and tightened. Together, the wood and rope created such a secure fit that the boat was completely watertight!

This tomb painting shows an ancient Egyptian sailboat.

In total, one mile of rope was originally used to connect Khufu's ship's wooden pieces. The rope was made from strands of tough grass that were braided together.

A Ship for the Afterlife

It took Youssef about ten years of hard work to reconstruct the ancient ship. When his work was completed, the ship looked just as it had thousands of years before. Yet the question remained—why had the magnificent craft been buried alongside Pharaoh Khufu's pyramid? One possible explanation involves the ancient Egyptians' strong belief in the **afterlife**.

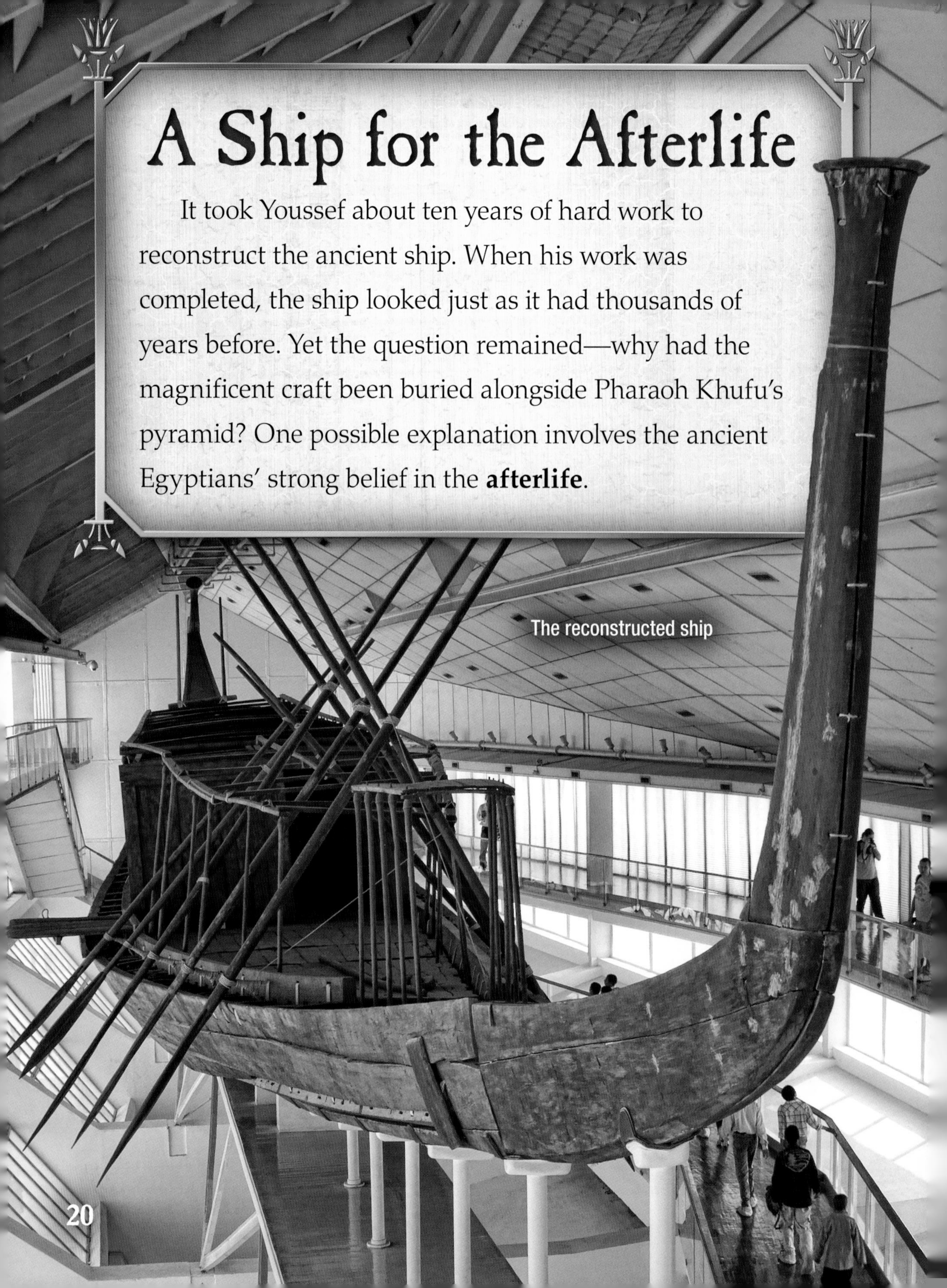

The reconstructed ship

The ancient Egyptians believed that after death, a person's **spirit** lived on in the afterlife. In order for this to happen, a person's body had to be preserved and made into a **mummy**. Then the mummy was laid in a tomb with everything his or her spirit might need in the afterlife, such as food and small boats for traveling. When a pharaoh died, however, he had a different journey to make. For his trip, he needed a very special boat.

To make a mummy, a body was dried out and then wrapped in linen bandages.

A model boat from the tomb of Pharaoh Tutankhamen

The ancient Egyptians had many different ideas about the afterlife. One belief was that a person might live on in the "Field of Reeds." In this lush **paradise**, there were rivers filled with boats and fields of crops.

Traveling with Ra

The ancient Egyptians worshipped many different gods. Their most important god was Ra, the sun god and creator of the world. Every morning, the sun, or Ra, rose in the east. Throughout the day, Ra traveled through the skies on a boat called a solar barque. Then, as the sun set in the west, Ra died. Throughout the night, Ra sailed through a dark place called the underworld. Then the sun god rose into the sky again the next morning.

A tomb painting showing the sun god Ra riding on a solar barque

The ancient Egyptians believed their pharaoh was a god who lived on Earth. Once the pharaoh died, he would sail through the skies with Ra. Many **Egyptologists** think that Pharaoh Khufu's ship is meant to be a solar barque. It was buried alongside the pharaoh's tomb so he could sail with Ra for all eternity.

In ancient Egypt, the west was a place of death because the sun set, or died, there each night. The bodies of the dead were transported by boat across the Nile to be buried in the west. This final journey across the river **symbolized** a person moving to the land of the dead.

A model of a funeral barge carrying a mummy

A Race Against Time

When Al-Mallakh discovered Khufu's ship in 1954, he also found a second closed-up pit. When this pit was investigated in the 1980s, archaeologists discovered that it, too, contained a wooden ship. In 2013, the excavation of this ship began. Unfortunately, the team is in a race against time. Unlike the first ship, the ancient wood of the second ship is rotting. It is also being damaged by insects and mold.

A team of archaeologists remove pieces of the second ancient ship from its pit

To safely remove the ship from the pit, a team of archaeologists wear hooded suits to make sure they do not further harm the timbers. As each piece of the ship is removed from the pit, digital photos are taken of the wood. These images will allow the scientists to plan a reconstruction. They will be able to test ways to rebuild the ship on a computer without needing to touch the delicate wood.

An archaeologist works to protect a 4,500-year-old wooden beam from the second ship.

Inside both boat pits, archaeologists discovered **cartouches**. A cartouche has an oval frame and contains symbols called **hieroglyphs**. The hieroglyphs in the boat pit cartouches spell out the names of Khufu and his son Djedefre.

Khufu's cartouche

The Ghost Ship

Pharaoh Khufu's ship has revealed many secrets about ancient Egyptian boat building. One mystery still remains to be solved, however. What was the true purpose of the magnificent wooden ship? Was it designed to carry the pharaoh through the skies with Ra? Or was it actually a boat that carried the pharaoh along the River Nile during his lifetime? For now, the experts cannot agree. Perhaps one day more **evidence** will be found that will help solve the mystery.

Today, the reconstructed ship is on display in Egypt. It stands in a museum that was specially built above the area where the boat was found.

The boat museum near the Great Pyramid

For more than 4,500 years, the ship lay hidden beneath sand and rock. Now, like a ghost, Pharaoh Khufu's ship has risen from the desert to sail on forever.
The reconstructed ship is 144 feet (44 m) long. Its stern (back) and bow (front) were carved to look like papyrus stalks.
The bow
The stern

Egypt's Ancient Secrets

The Egyptologists who studied Pharaoh Khufu's ship have lots of theories about its secret past, but many mysteries remain.

Was the Ship a Funeral Barge?

Once Pharaoh Khufu's mummy was prepared, it would have been transported from the ancient Egyptian city of Memphis to the Great Pyramid at Giza. Some experts think the ship was a funeral barge that carried Khufu's mummy on its final journey along the Nile. The king's mummy would have been laid out inside the barge's deckhouse.

What Happened to the Missing Ships?

Archaeologists have found five boat pits around the base of the Great Pyramid. Three of the pits were empty, though. Did these pits once hold wooden ships, too? One theory is that the holes were never made to hold boats. The boat shapes may have been carved into the rock to symbolize ships.

An empty boat pit

Why Did Khufu Need Five Boats?

No one knows for sure, but some experts think that four of the boats were designed to be used in the afterlife. These boats would carry the pharaoh in the four directions of the universe—north, east, south, and west. The fifth boat might have been used in real life to carry Pharaoh Khufu's mummy to the Great Pyramid.

afterlife (AF-tur-*life*) the life a person has after he or she dies

archaeologist (*ar*-kee-OL-uh-jist) a scientist who learns about ancient times by studying things he or she digs up

artifacts (ART-uh-*fakts*) objects of historical interest that were made by people

canopy (KAN-uh-pee) a covering

cartouches (kahr-TOOSH-is) oval-shaped carvings or paintings that contain hieroglyphic writing

civilization (siv-*uh*-luh-ZAY-shuhn) a highly developed society

Egyptologists (ee-jip-TOL-uh-jists) historians or scientists who study ancient Egypt

evidence (EV-uh-duhnss) objects or information used to prove something

excavating (*eks*-kuh-VAYT-ing) uncovering or digging up

fertile (FUR-tal) filled with nutrients that plants need for growth and health

hieroglyphs (HYE-ur-uh-*glifs*) pictures used in Egyptian writing

mummy (MUH-mee) the preserved body of a dead person

nutrients (NUH-tree-uhnts) substances that plants need to grow and be healthy

oar (OHR) a pole with a flat blade, used for rowing or steering a boat through water

papyrus (puh-PYE-ruhss) a tall plant that grows in water; strips of papyrus stems were used to make paper in ancient Egypt

paradise (PA-ruh-dice) a place of great beauty, peace, and joy

pharaoh (FAIR-oh) a ruler of ancient Egypt

plaster (PLAS-tur) a material used in construction; it's made from powdered rock, sand, and water

quarries (KWOR-eez) places in the ground where large rocks are cut

reconstruct (ree-kuhn-STRUK) to rebuild something

restoring (ri-STAWR-ing) cleaning or repairing something old to make it look new again

spirit (SPIHR-it) the part of a person that may live on after death

symbolized (SIM-buh-lahyzd) stood for or represented something else

timber (TIM-bur) wood used for building things

tomb (TOOM) a grave, room, or building in which a dead body is buried

torrent (TAWR-uhnt) a strong, rushing stream of water

vessel (VES-uhl) a ship or large boat

Bibliography

Romer, John. *Ancient Lives: Daily Life in Egypt of the Pharaohs.* New York: Holt, Rinehart, and Winston (1984).

Romer, John. *The Great Pyramid: Ancient Egypt Revisited.* Cambridge, UK: Cambridge University Press (2007).

Read More

Boyer, Crispin. *Everything Ancient Egypt (National Geographic Kids).* Washington, DC: National Geographic (2012).

Kaplan, Leslie C. *Technology of Ancient Egypt (Primary Sources of Ancient Civilizations).* New York: Rosen (2004).

Owen, Ruth. *How to Make an Egyptian Mummy (It's a Fact!).* New York: Ruby Tuesday Books (2015).

Learn More Online

To learn more about the ghost ship, visit
www.bearportpublishing.com/EgyptsAncientSecrets

Index

About the Author

Ruth Owen has written many nonfiction books for children. She has always been fascinated by ancient Egyptian history and the work of archaeologists.